# LOVE LETTERS TO GOD

30 DAYS OF STRENGTHENING AND BUILDING A
CLOSER RELATIONSHIP WITH GOD

ALAINA D HUNT

Love Letters to God: 30 Days of Strengthening and
Building a Closer Relationship with God.
Copyright © 2021 by Alaina Hunt.

All rights reserved. Printed in the United States of America. No part of this book may be used or reproduced in any manner whatsoever without written permission except in the case of brief quotations embodied in critical articles and reviews. Permission granted on request.

Qui 2 Life Publishing
Hamilton Center II
3261 Old Washington Road, Suite 2020
Waldorf, MD 20602
www.qui2life.com
1 (301) 710-5219

Print ISBN: 978-1-7326177-9-7

eBook ISBN: 978-1-7326177-7-3

Library of Congress Cataloging-in-Publication

Author Name: Alaina Hunt

Title: Love Letters to God: 30 Days of Strengthening and Building a Closer Relationship with God

Edited by: Tonitta Hopkins and T. Lynn Tate

Cover Design by SPJ Graphics

Qui 2 Life Publishing is not responsible for any content or determination of work. All information is solely considered as the point of view of the author.

Scriptures taken from Holy Bible, King James Version®, Copyright ©1973, 1978, 1984, 2011 by Biblica, Inc.® Used by permission. All rights reserved worldwide.

*This book is dedicated to my Daddy, Jacob Johnson, and my Mama, Rhonda Johnson. Thank you for teaching me dedication, hard work, perseverance, long suffering, and to see the best side of people and situations. If it weren't for you teaching me the ways of God and being holy examples, I would not be here! Thank you!*

# ACKNOWLEDGMENTS

Without God, I truly would not be in any position to tell of how great He is. I thank God for sending His son, Jesus, to die so I might live. If it wasn't for this gift of new life, I (we) would have absolutely no hope!

I would like to thank my husband, Maurice Hunt, for not only being that push for me to go forth in what God has birthed in me but to keep going and complete the mission. I appreciate, love, and thank you!

I want to thank my four children, Simone, Stephen, Shane, and Salena, for being such a joy to my life and for being troopers adapting to everything we have gone through. As we adapted, we overcame it all with the help of the Lord. You all are a big part of me! I love each one of you!

I must thank my parents, Jacob and Rhonda Johnson, for their love, encouragement, and example throughout my life. Leading me to Jesus, praying me through, being that living example that is so needed in this day--strong parents, standing united, and fighting through prayer. I honor you both!

I also would like to thank my spiritual leaders, Pastor Willie R. Hunt and First Lady JoAnn Hunt. I am grateful for the relationship that we have. Thank you for being real, teaching me the word of God, and mentoring me throughout all these years by precept and example. You taught me balance, which is so needed in these days. I am also grateful to God for bringing not only you into my life, but your oldest son who made you not only my Pastor and First Lady, but also my Mom and Dad.

To my family and friends, I pray for you, I love you, and I bless you. Praying we all get ready, be ready and stay ready, in Jesus' name, Amen.

To you, the people of God who see the importance of growing in God! We must keep our relationship with him first and foremost in our hearts and minds. Let's win through this life victoriously through God's word and seek to do his will until we meet on that distant shore, in glory! Nothing is more important than where we will spend eternity. So, let's get Heaven ready!

# THE JOURNEY BEGINS

# DAY 1

Father,
You are my delight! I long to be in your presence and in your peace! Thank you for your love towards me. My desire is to be who and what you would have me to be. I don't want to be so busy that I get sucked in a rhythm of mindlessly doing "things," and miss out on loving you!

You are the source of my strength--the lamp and light unto my feet. I depend on you to lead and guide me. What a waste if I am a "things" person and not a God person. I don't want to be like Martha, incumbent about many things, but not at your feet when you are near. Draw me close and your presence will be my delight! Your word will be my comfort and your Holy Ghost my guide.

Jesus, I long for you. May the longing for you always be first and foremost in my heart. My heart screams YES to your will and your way! Your presence is my delight, and I desire to make you smile and proud of me. I give you permission to shape my life that it may bring glory to your name.

## Meditative Moment

Have you ever felt like you needed to stop every carnal thing in your life and run to the bosom of Jesus? We must continually pray to be in the right relationship with the Father. Not a surface relationship, but a deeper level that He can engage with us and be pleased with our lives. Today, take an assessment of the things that keep you busy and distracted from spending quality time in God's presence. Then decide three things you will do to improve your quality time with God.

## Prayer

Father God, in the name of Jesus, we want to know you in a more intimate way. We recognize the importance of relationship and open our hearts to receive more of you. It doesn't matter if we "say" we know you, if you never knew us. Father, we want you to know our names. Commune with us and change us for the better. Our desire is to be in the center of your will--right where you want us to be. In Jesus' mighty and sweet name, we pray, Amen.

> "Delight thyself also in the LORD; And he shall give thee the desires of thine heart."
> Psalm 37:4 KJV

# DAILY REFLECTIONS

*Today I am grateful for...*

_____

_____

_____

*Today's message reminded that...*

_____

_____

_____

*Today I will strengthen my relationship with God by...*

_____

_____

_____

# DAY 2

Father,
I need your help! I know church work is necessary. Just as with a business, there are programs, administration, finance meetings, etc. The work must be done so that things run smoothly. But, when leaders won't and others don't, when do I get to say enough is enough? I'm constantly reminded that only what we do for you, God, will last; but what do I do when the work is just too much?

Help me Lord to find balance in you. I need your guidance and direction. I need a correct balance of work time, play time, and intimacy time. I don't want the work and play time to outweigh our intimacy time, and I know that DEPENDS on me. Help me Lord! Help me to push everything else aside so that WE can commune together.

Five virgins were wise, meaning they were productive and worked to store up. They were saved because of their wisdom. Then there were 5 more virgins that were not wise.

They were foolish and did not store up causing them to perish. I want to be wise! Wise in my decisions and wise in my relationship with you. I put my hands on my head and ask you right now for wisdom to know and to grow in you. Help me Jesus!

### Meditative Moment

Do you sometimes feel like you may not be in right standing with our Lord and savior? Feeling like you may not be all the way right in your thoughts and actions? Let's look to the Lord and ask Him to help us grow and push towards His everlasting arms. He is our only hope and help!

Today meditate and ask God to show you what HE wants you to do, and how HE wants you to do it. Ask Him to show you how HE wants you to go up and out for His Glory. Push all the "stuff" aside and talk to Jesus!

### Prayer

Father, in the name of Jesus, we come to you now with an open heart, an open mind, and an open spirit asking you to lead and guide us through establishing the perfect balance for our lives. We don't want to be so comfortable doing things our way that we get off course. As we put our hands on our head, we pray for wisdom, guidance, and understanding. Teach us your ways so we won't sin against you. Help us, in Jesus' name, Amen.

"A false balance is abomination to the LORD:
But a just weight is his delight."
Proverbs 11:1 KJV

# DAILY REFLECTIONS

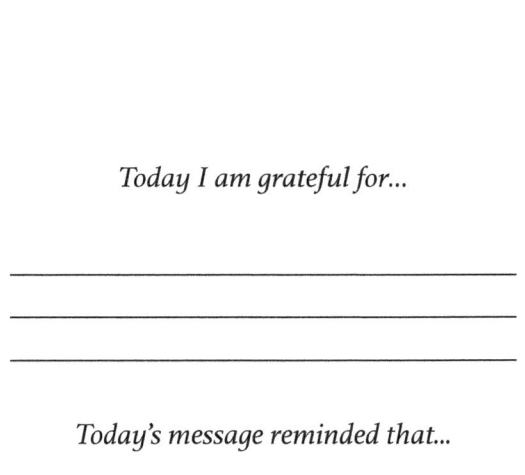

*Today I am grateful for...*

_____
_____
_____

*Today's message reminded that...*

_____
_____
_____

*Today I will strengthen my relationship with God by...*

_____
_____
_____

# DAY 3

Father,
There is a sense of urgency in the land, our churches, our homes, and communities. I know you long for me to be in your presence more. So, I set the intentions of my heart and mind to be in your presence like never before. I give you permission to take me to a place in you that I have never been before. It is impossible for me to have the desire unless you put it in me.

I seek you with all my heart, soul, mind, and spirit--all of me. I give you everything, and say YES to your plan, your will, and to your way! Create in me a heart of worship. Develop in me a "go forth" spirit! I want to serve you with joy and gladness. Know me through and through, and if you find any wicked way in me, take it out and make me new. Deliver me from any evil desires, ways, or thoughts. I desire to push into another dimension in you.

## Meditative Moment

Do you ever feel like you worship God on a surface level? You desire more, but you don't know how to go further in your prayers and worship. Let's commit to jumping in and going deeper than we've ever gone before in God. God is everything we ever needed or wanted. So, we ask, we seek, we knock, and we allow Him to take us to the place in Him where he desires us to be.

Today, take time to close your eyes and concentrate on God. Shut out all the distractions and go deeper in your prayers and experience with God. Say YES to intimate worship with God!

## Prayer

Lord, help us to surrender all to you. Help us in our inner most parts to first believe, then to know that you are our source and strength. We trust that you will never leave us nor forsake us. We are here awaiting your manifested presence. Cleanse us Lord of anything that is not pleasing to you that our worship may be pure in your sight. In Jesus' precious name, Amen.

> "But it is good for me to draw near to God: I have put my trust in the Lord GOD, That I may declare all thy works."
> Psalm 73:28 KJV

# DAILY REFLECTIONS

*Today I am grateful for...*

_____
_____
_____

*Today's message reminded that...*

_____
_____
_____

*Today I will strengthen my relationship with God by...*

_____
_____
_____

# DAY 4

Father,
   Draw me close to you. All throughout the day, may I meditate on your goodness and grace. I want to honor your name with every fiber of my being. I will glorify you in my walk, in my talk, and as I go about my day. May my demeanor, conversations, and attitude be a reflection of you. How can I be a representative of you if I don't reflect you?

You do not operate in hate, selfishness, or blame. Instead, you are kind, long suffering and patient. You do not want me or any of your children to perish. You want me to be free in you. So here I am, humbling submitting myself to be one with you.

You have done great things for me. There is safety, covering, and provision in your great shadow. Therefore, I abide in you, your will, and your way. You allow me free will, and I choose to walk with you each day of my life. I choose to draw in close to you, and I choose to serve you, the Most High

God, with a cheerful heart. Who can compare to you and your great love?

## Meditative Moment

Listen, God is a gentleman. He does not go against our will. We must give God permission to take over in our lives and our hearts. We should make an effort daily to stay in the will of the Father that he may be pleased with our lives.

Today, let's take note of what may be hindering us from growing in our relationship with the Father. What steps can we take to remove these blocks and press into his presence?

## Prayer

Father, in the name of Jesus, help us to stay under your safety! Lead and guide us along our journey that we may be where you'd have us to be. You are a great protector and an awesome Savior! We want to reverence you. We are reliant on your light unto our path, for it is our compass to the abundant life you have promised. Thank you for the privilege to come boldly into your presence and speak with you. The safety of your arms, your will, and your way is what we long for, in Jesus' name, Amen.

> "The Lord is not slack concerning his promise, as some men count slackness; but is longsuffering to us-ward, not willing that any should perish, but that all should come to repentance."
> 2 Peter 3:9 KJV

# DAILY REFLECTIONS

*Today I am grateful for...*

_____
_____
_____

*Today's message reminded that...*

_____
_____
_____

*Today I will strengthen my relationship with God by...*

_____
_____
_____

# DAY 5

Father,
Thank you for the opportunity to come before you. Early in the morning do I seek your face! You desire my discipline and diligence meeting you each day. Prompt and poised I'm ready to hear from you. I understand the intentionality that is needed in this relationship.

One might wonder, "Why do you want me to rise and meet you each day? Can't I just stay in my bed and mouth a few words of thanks and go back to sleep? I mean, you know all and see all anyway. Why do I have to be diligent and disciplined?" I believe just as you are dependable and intentional with me, you want the same things of me.

Just as in a romantic relationship, the excitement and preparation I give a mere human being should be that much more for the one who died for my sins. You are the one who keeps me alive and has the power to save or destroy my soul. This coming together should not be out of fear of going to hell, but one of love and appreciation for who you are and all the provisions you've made and continue to make on my behalf.

### Meditative Moment

Think back on a time when you had a crush on someone. Remember the excitement and jitters you felt in the pit of your stomach? What about the attention to detail you applied as you prepared to see them? Well, our Lord and Savior would love that same joy, preparation, love, and attention as if he were your crush. Wow! What an eye-opening way to think about our encounter with God.

Today, let's give thanks to God for how he has kept us and continuously expresses his love for us. What ways can you show God just how much you are "crushing" on him today?

### Prayer

Father God, in the name of Jesus, let our love for you grow more and more each day--never dulling, never getting stale, never loosing stamina but always staying true, vibrant, and adventurous. We want to know the depths of your ways and serve you with gladness. What a wonderful God you are! We love and adore you and long for more of you. In Jesus' name, Amen.

"O God, thou art My God; early will I seek thee: My soul

thirsteth for thee, my flesh longeth for thee in a dry and thirsty land, where no water is."
Psalm 63:1 KJV

# DAILY REFLECTIONS

*Today I am grateful for...*

_____
_____
_____

*Today's message reminded that...*

_____
_____
_____

*Today I will strengthen my relationship with God by...*

_____
_____
_____

# DAY 6

Father,
R.E.A.L. That's what you are to me. You are relating, exciting, all-knowing, and loving. The true depths of your ways provoke me to an exploration of you as if on a treasure hunt. What plans do you have for me, oh God? Your word reminds me that you have plans to prosper and not harm me. The love you show towards me second by second, tending to my every feeling and thought—the pushing, pulling, tugging and willingness to help me so that I won't perish!

What an awesome God you are! You know all things, hear all things, and see all things. I praise and bless your name for being real with me. So, I in return desire to be real with you. Thank you, Jesus for that desire.

## Meditative Moment

R.E.A.L. There are so many wonderful and beautiful things about our God. What adjectives can you come up with to describe God? Take some time to reflect on your life and how God has opened doors, closed doors, changed the entire trajectory of your personal course. Take in how loving and intentional He is with your life.

## Prayer

Father, thank you! Thank you for always keeping it R.E.A.L. with us, and for laying out the blueprint in your word for us to follow. We appreciate you and the REALness of what's to come if we obey or disobey your word. You, God, are intentional. We thank and praise you and ask for your help to become the best version of ourselves, in Jesus' name, Amen.

> "For I know the thoughts that I think toward you, saith the LORD, thoughts of peace, and not of evil, to give you an expected end. Then shall ye call upon me, and ye shall go and pray unto me, and I will hearken unto you. And ye shall seek me, and find me, when ye shall search for me with all your heart."
> Jeremiah 29:11-13 KJV

# DAILY REFLECTIONS

*Today I am grateful for...*

_____
_____
_____

*Today's message reminded that...*

_____
_____
_____

*Today I will strengthen my relationship with God by...*

_____
_____
_____

## DAY 7

Father,
You want to be my heart's desire—to be close in relationship with me that I may share my inner most thoughts and feelings with you without reservation or fear. You want to be acknowledged and consulted for the solutions to my life's problems. It's your desire for me to be one after your own heart—seeking you for the who, what, when, and how. I am striving and pushing to draw close to you Father. I don't want this world and these temporary situations to distract and draw me away from you.

Closer, closer, closer is where I truly want to be and stay. May I always be open in communication with you from the depths of my heart. Be pleased with my life and take joy in my service. Pleasing you is my heart's desire. Help me Lord to be more like you.

## Meditative Moment

Don't you want to go "all in" with God the Father, no distractions, no interruptions, and no holding back? Even if you're not at that point just yet, ask God for a heart to want to go "all in" with Him.

Today, let's reflect on what may be preventing us from going all in with God. Is it a person, a job, a past hurt, a misunderstanding? Whatever it may be, we can talk to God about it and ask Him for His help to lay it aside that we may go deeper in God.

## Prayer

Father God, help us! We want to jump all in for you. Teach us your ways, in Jesus' name Amen.

> "One thing have I desired of the LORD, that will I seek after; That I may dwell in the house of the LORD all the days of my life, to beholdthe beauty of the LORD, and to enquire in his temple."
> Psalm 27:4 KJV

# DAILY REFLECTIONS

*Today I am grateful for...*

_____
_____
_____

*Today's message reminded that...*

_____
_____
_____

*Today I will strengthen my relationship with God by...*

_____
_____
_____

# DAY 8

Father,
Although I may not make an impact on THE world, I can make an impact on MY world with you, Lord, with me every single step of the way! I trust you to order my steps that I may impact those who cross my path! I desire to influence, impact, and provoke positive change in their lives for the BETTER!!! Lord, you make my life better and I want to be a reflection of you and your love. I want to inspire others to trust your plan for their lives that they may experience the true meaning of BETTER—better thoughts, better decisions, and better living.

## Meditative Moment

Have you ever considered how you can make a difference in the world around you, but got discouraged because you didn't see how your small effort would affect the bigger picture? Take the first step by focusing on and helping those that are around you.

Today, let's think of creative and innovative ways to share the love of Christ with those that cross our paths. We don't have to save the whole world at once. We can make a difference in our world, one person at a time.

## Prayer

Lord, help us understand that we don't have to save the entire world. As we become a reflection of you, we will encourage others to do the same. Together we will spread your love around the world. In Jesus' name, Amen.

> "The steps of a good man are ordered by the LORD: And he delighteth in his way."
> Psalm 37:23 KJV

# DAILY REFLECTIONS

*Today I am grateful for...*

_____
_____
_____

*Today's message reminded that...*

_____
_____
_____

*Today I will strengthen my relationship with God by...*

_____
_____
_____

# DAY 9

Father,
I have come to realize that every decision I make affects not only me, but someone else's life, as well. One decision, good or bad, can change the entire trajectory of one's life. Sometimes I'm not even aware of others that may have been affected by my decision or even how it may have impacted them. I think about those that didn't choose you, but instead chose material things and people. They're now paying the price either on this earth, or on the other side of their life.

I set my intentions to make good and sound decisions for my life. While I know I can't live my life for others, I don't want to be the cause for someone else's fall. If I am not careful, I can become a stumbling block for those that are in search and need of you. I want to be a great representation of you, Lord. I surrender my will to you and ask that you help me do better!

## Meditative Moment

Have you ever thought about how your actions and decisions affect the lives of those around you? While we shouldn't consume ourselves with other's opinions of us, we can't allow our actions to compromise our witness to those in search of Christ.

Today, let's take an assessment of the decisions we've been making and the impact they've had on our witness for Christ. From this day, let's set our intention to have the mind of Christ and be a reflection of his love every day.

## Prayer

Lord Help us!!! In Jesus' name Amen.

> "Let your light so shine before men, that they may see your good works, and glorify your Father which is in heaven."
> Matthew 5:16 KJV

# DAILY REFLECTIONS

*Today I am grateful for...*

_____
_____
_____

*Today's message reminded that...*

_____
_____
_____

*Today I will strengthen my relationship with God by...*

_____
_____
_____

# DAY 10

Father,
I thank you for life! You have allowed me the opportunity, once again, to give you praise on this side of Heaven, and I thank you. The absolute beauty of your creation is superb. The orchestration of it all is mind blowing and undeniably the most magnificent thing I have ever seen. You have set everything in motion! You did it! What a wonderful savior you are!

I reverence you for your greatness! Words cannot describe how glorious you are. No word in the human language truly captures the essence and depth of your Majesty. So, for now I will simply give you the highest praise. HALLELUJAH! YOU alone are worthy to be praised! YOU alone are worthy of my worship! YOU alone are worthy of the glory from my LIFE!!! Oh, how I love you Jesus!

## Meditative Moment

Have you ever been to a place that left you in awe of its beauty—a place with landscapes that truly were a wonder? God is so magnificent and took his time creating the foundations of this world. But too often we miss the opportunity to take in and savor the beauty and glory of his creation. Just as he created this world, he put the same time and attention into creating you.

Today, stop and take in God's beautiful creation around you. Journal your praise and appreciation for God's splendor.

## Prayer

Father, in the name of Jesus, we thank and praise you for your loving kindness and wonderful mercies that are new every morning! Why? Because you have our best interest at heart. Our love and adoration we freely give to you. May we love and appreciate you the way you desire and never stop believing in your excellency. In Jesus' mighty and matchless name, we pray, Amen!

> "For the invisible things of him from the creation of the world
> are clearly seen, being understood by the things that are made, even his eternal power and Godhead; so that
> they are without excuse:"
> Romans 1:20 KJV

# DAILY REFLECTIONS

*Today I am grateful for...*

_____
_____
_____

*Today's message reminded that...*

_____
_____
_____

*Today I will strengthen my relationship with God by...*

_____
_____
_____

# DAY 11

Father,
What a beautiful and sweet savior I have in YOU, Jesus! You love me more than I could ever know, and it is more than I can even fathom in my own understanding. What a beautiful blessing it is for me to be in your presence and a part of your family. I thank you! I thank you! I thank you! Yes, over, and over, I say thank you!

When I look back over my life, I see the many times you spared me. You granted me grace when I put myself in difficult situations, but there were many who lost their lives for far less. I give you praise for your continued mercies! Grace upon grace you've given to me and those around me—oh the sovereignty. What a beautiful blessing it is to be called your child. I love and appreciate you for your loving kindness!

### Meditative Moment

When was the last time you took time to reflect on God's mercy toward your life? How many times has He spared you from accidents, mishaps, and total devastation? What a faithful and magnificent God we serve.

Today, reflect back on the times that the blessing of God's mercy spared you and journal your reflections giving God his due praise.

### Prayer

Father, we give you praise and glory as we remember what could have been, but you kept us safe even when we didn't deserve to be kept. We love you and appreciate you! Let our love for you grow stronger and deeper! Help us to freely dive into your love, and allow more of you and less of us trying to control our own lives. We know we can never repay the debt that we owe you. Therefore, we surrender our will and selves completely to you. In Jesus' name, Amen.

> "The LORD bless thee, and keep thee: The LORD make his face shine upon thee, and be gracious unto thee: The LORD lift up his countenance upon thee, and give thee peace."
> Numbers 6:24-26 KJV

# DAILY REFLECTIONS

*Today I am grateful for...*

_____
_____
_____

*Today's message reminded that...*

_____
_____
_____

*Today I will strengthen my relationship with God by...*

_____
_____
_____

# DAY 12

Father,

Faith! Trusting you, God, through every situation. Faith! Believing you, God, in every circumstance! Faith! Knowing that everything is already alright because you have left everything on record, in Your word, for me to stand on. I read your word. I believe your word, and I stand on your word!

Father, I have the faith to believe you for everything! You said that if I can muster up a little faith, even as small as a mustard seed, that alone would be enough to push me through whatever situation I may find myself. I have faith in you, God! Yes Lord! I have faith in Your word! Yes Lord! I have faith in Your plan God! Yes Lord! I trust you Lord and have confidence in You! I stretch out in You, Oh God! I activate my faith through Jesus Christ! FAITH!

## Meditative Moment

In life, we will have disappointing moments. People will let us down. People will lie on us. People will even talk about us. As "good" as we think we are, they will find something to say negative about us. Yes, they sure will! But let us make up in our minds that we don't have to respond to everything that is said about us or to us. Let's do like Jesus did. When they accused Him, he was quiet and did not give them what they deserved. Instead, He extended mercy.

Today, have faith in the spirit of God within you and stand on God's word. Be mindful of your responses when people try to frustrate or discourage you. Remember, God is faithful and in him alone should we place our faith and trust.

## Prayer

Father, you see and you know when someone is sent to discourage and distract us from the path you have set for us. Help us to not be swift to anger, but mindful of our responses. May we operate in your wisdom and strength throughout our day. In Jesus' name, Amen.

"And Jesus answering saith unto them, Have faith in God. For verily I say unto you, That whosoever shall say unto this mountain, Be thou removed, and be thou cast into the sea; and shall not doubt in his heart, but shall believe that those things which he saith shall come to pass; he shall have whatsoever he saith. Therefore I say unto you, What things soever ye desire, when ye pray, believe that ye receive them, and ye shall have them."

Mark 11:22-24 KJV

# DAILY REFLECTIONS

*Today I am grateful for...*

_____
_____
_____

*Today's message reminded that...*

_____
_____
_____

*Today I will strengthen my relationship with God by...*

_____
_____
_____

## DAY 13

Father,
You are the creator of all things, and you desire quality time with me daily. Wow! How humbling it is to know that the One who was, is, and is to come would pursue a beautiful healthy and blossoming relationship with little ole' me. You know every hair on my head and every thought I have without me saying it. You are the best friend anyone could ever ask.

I love you Father! What a beautiful blessing it is to be awaken for "intimate time" in your presence! A time to talk to you and hear you clearly through the reading of your word! I honor our flourishing relationship and you as the Lord over my life! I just want to be pleasing and acceptable in your eyes. You sacrificed your son, Jesus, for me, and in exchange I give you my life, my time, my thoughts, my everything. You are amazing! Everything I do is for your Glory.

## Meditative Moment

God knows every intricate detail about us. From the very innocent thoughts that we had in our mother's womb to our last breath. He desires us to know him just as intricately—the desires of his heart for our lives.

Today in your prayer time ask God to share with you his heart's desire for your life and that you will have the courage to pursue it with your whole heart.

## Prayer

Father God, in the name of Jesus, as we go throughout our day, we ask that you walk and talk with us along the way. Help us to see and hear you clearly in all that we do. Purify our hearts and sanctify us that we may serve out your divine purpose for our lives. In Jesus' mighty name, Amen.

"Create in me a clean heart, O God; And renew a right spirit within me. Cast me not away from thy presence; And take not thy holy spirit from me. Restore unto me the joy of thy salvation; And uphold me with thy free spirit."
Psalm 51:10-12 KJV

# DAILY REFLECTIONS

*Today I am grateful for...*

_____
_____
_____

*Today's message reminded that...*

_____
_____
_____

*Today I will strengthen my relationship with God by...*

_____
_____
_____

# DAY 14

Father,
 Thank you for your word! On days when I am weary, Your word provides nourishment for my spirit. I know that the process comes to grow me, prune me, and shape me. It's uncomfortable, but necessary so that I may become who you have created me to be. Daily I count to remind myself, "1,2,3 trust God; 4,5,6 believe God; 7,8,9 have faith in God!"

The faith I have in YOUR plan MUST outweigh the pain of the process. There is no failure in you, therefore I cannot fail. I put my total trust in you and the process as I continue to walk in it and through it with you. Thank you for always having my back.

## Meditative Moment

Have you ever been in a situation where you totally didn't understand why you were going through a situation? In everything, we must truly ensure that our hearts and minds are fixed on Jesus and His plan, knowing that nothing He ever does is wasted. Every word He speaks has purpose and is intentional.

Today, meditate on the many times God has brought you out of situations that you thought you would never make it through, and know that if he did it before he will do it again.

## Prayer

Father, in the name of Jesus, help me to trust the process and your plan for MY life! Comparing myself to others, but not knowing what they've had to go through is pointless. Today, I commit to the process even when I don't understand or have all the answers. May you get the glory from my life as I find joy and peace in you. Thank you Father, in Jesus' name Amen.

> "Trust in the LORD with all thine heart; And lean not unto thine own understanding. In all thy ways acknowledge him, And he shall direct thy paths."
> Proverbs 3:5-6 KJV

# DAILY REFLECTIONS

*Today I am grateful for...*

_____
_____
_____

*Today's message reminded that...*

_____
_____
_____

*Today I will strengthen my relationship with God by...*

_____
_____
_____

# DAY 15

Father,
Taking time to sit still and hear what you have to say can sometimes be a difficult thing, especially if I'm doing all the talking. Help me to be more aware of when I am doing more talking than listening. There is peace in the stillness. Often, I wonder if that's what you're trying to tell me, "Be Still."

The stillness allows time for reflection and reverence of you and your greatness. Jesus, I adore you! Let my heart worship you in the stillness of time. Let my soul rest in your wonderful greatness for you are beautiful, you are great, and you are worthy to be worshipped and adored. Let my heart stretch out to yours. Let me lean on you for guidance along this journey with grace. What do you want to say to my heart today? I am here still and listening.

## Meditative Moment

Sometimes we must stop, sit still, and wait. God is not on our time; we are on His. He is the creator of time. Let's confidently spend time sitting still in His presence, awaiting His clear instructions.

Today throughout your day, set aside 2- 3 minutes to sit still in a quiet place and concentrate on God. Is He speaking to your heart? What do you hear in your spirit? Write it down.

## Prayer

Father, in Jesus' name, help us to wait on you. May we reflect upon your wonderful greatness and sit still long enough for you to speak. Help us not to be in a hurry to speak and do, but willing to stay still and wait on you. We absolutely appreciate you and want to be closer to you. In Jesus' name Amen.

> "Be still, and know that I am God: I will be exalted among the heathen, I will be exalted in the earth."
> Psalm 46:10 KJV

# DAILY REFLECTIONS

*Today I am grateful for...*

_____
_____
_____

*Today's message reminded that...*

_____
_____
_____

*Today I will strengthen my relationship with God by...*

_____
_____
_____

# DAY 16

Father,
 I want to fall in love with you over and over again, not because of what you can do for me, but because you are the sovereign Lord of All. You've created a beautiful world for us to enjoy. Although we have not always upkept the land as you intended, I'm grateful for the beautiful places that remain, and you've allowed us to enjoy! You are just awesome! You are good great!!! Yes, I said good great because our words truly cannot explain the vastness of your goodness!

All of this you have done for us. The day I can see you as you are, for myself, oh what a glorious day! To see the One I've been hearing about my whole life. The One who I've been praying to cleanse, fix, and save me. Lord, Jesus, what a most blessed day that reunion will be. To behold the beauty of who you truly are, oh what a day that will be!

Jesus, I must get Heaven ready! I don't want to miss this

train! I give you permission to take control of my life so that I will be ready when you return. My answer is Yes! Yes Lord! Yes Lord! YES!

## Meditative Moment

Have you ever sat back and thought about how wonderful Heaven is? How grand it will be when we get there. I know I do. Do you think about the flowers singing, the clear rivers running through beautiful trees, and colors we cannot even describe? Oh, what a beautiful reunion it will be! Jesus the savior sitting right next to the Father, and we're all joined together in him.

Today, take a moment to think about what it will be like to be with the Father in Heaven. Then meditate on what it means to you to be Heaven ready and journal what you need to do to prepare for our Savior's return.

## Prayer

Father, in the name of Jesus, we give you permission to clean us up and straighten out our lives so we can be ready when you call us. We don't have the true capacity of thought or vocabulary to understand truly what that means to be with you. But Father, wherever you are, that's where we want to be. So, save us from ourselves, and clean us from all unrighteousness. Keep us from evil thoughts, ways, and deeds. It is in Jesus' mighty name that we pray, Amen.

"One thing have I desired of the LORD, that will I seek after; That I may dwell in the house of the LORD all the days of my life, To behold the beauty of the LORD, and to enquire in his temple."
Psalm 27:4 KJV

# DAILY REFLECTIONS

*Today I am grateful for...*

_____
_____
_____

*Today's message reminded that...*

_____
_____
_____

*Today I will strengthen my relationship with God by...*

_____
_____
_____

# DAY 17

Father,
   Save me! Fill me, my entire being and every ounce of me, with your Holy Spirit so there is no room for anything that is not of you. I want to be filled to capacity leaving no room for the old me and old ways to creep back in stronger to destroy me. Save me and fill me Jesus! I want every single thing I do to represent you with the utmost honor, respect, and reverence!

On June 4, 1996, I raised my right hand in affirmation to defend these United States against all enemies foreign and domestic, to honor the flag, and to wear my service uniform with the utmost respect and honor. Today, I raise my hands to affirm that I will defend the gospel of Jesus Christ against all spiritual enemies, to honor God's word, and to unapologetically be a reflection of God's love with the utmost respect and honor! I surrender my life to you. Save me!

## Meditative Moment

We owe the God of all creation the upmost respect and reverence. Have you ever sat outside under the stars or looked online at the vastness of our universe? It's a reflection of God's infiniteness, and it's such a wonder. What's even greater is that same infinite God that created the heavens and the earth loves you; and if he could create such a wonder, how much more could he meet your needs? The only thing you have to do is submit yourself willingly and freely unto him.

Today, take a moment to go outside at nightfall and just take in the beauty of the night's sky. As you take it in, recommit yourself unto God and his will for your life. Know that if he can create this world, he can certainly fulfill your every need. Just trust him.

## Prayer

Father, in the name of Jesus, we thank you for the mind to ask you to save us. Drawing closer to you daily, we want nothing to come in between you and us! Help us to lay down everything that is not of you. We ask with a sincere heart, a humble spirit, and a renewed mind that you fill us with your Holy Spirit. Our lives are in your hands. You made us, and in total surrender we give you permission to make and mold us into who you purposed us to be in the first place. We continually yield to you over and over again. We thank you and trust you. In Jesus' name, Amen!

"Wherefore he is able also to save them to the uttermost that come unto God by him, seeing he ever liveth to make intercession for them."
Hebrews 7:25 KJV

# DAILY REFLECTIONS

*Today I am grateful for...*

_____
_____
_____

*Today's message reminded that...*

_____
_____
_____

*Today I will strengthen my relationship with God by...*

_____
_____
_____

# DAY 18

Father,
I long for you Jesus. In this evil and perverse world, I'm seeking and panting after you, your will, and your statues. I long to do right in your eyes, to be in your presence, and to follow your commands--holy and acceptable, not straddling the fence. Draw me deeper in you. You are the center of my joy!

Lord you are the comforter of my soul! You are the answer to all my questions. I pray that my life brings glory to you. Lord, I love you, and I love the fact that you first loved me. All that you ask of me is that I obey your precepts and commands.

Help me Lord JESUS! I want to always abound in your work and word and to please you every step of the way. You are my hope! I put my trust and cares in you. Be my peace, be my comfort, be my desire, and my everything. I love you Father!

### Meditative Moment

Are you living life God's way or your way? Most of the time we are busy living our lives and don't stop to consider how we're really living. If that's you, ask God to transform your heart so that your desire is to do it His way without compromise.

Today, make a new commitment to lay aside every weight and anything that tries to pull you away from the love of Jesus! The enemy of our souls can't stop what God has for us, but he can distract us and pull us off course if we allow it. Let's seek the LORD and his way of life for us with our whole heart so that we remain right with him.

### Prayer

Father God in the name of Jesus, thank you for this time to come to you in prayer and ask for your forgiveness. I ask for you to clean my heart and mind so that I may get and stay on the right path. Help me to desire life according to your purpose and plan for me. I say yes to your will and way even in the hard times, uneasy times, and happy and sad times. You are the only constant in my life. You are with me far beyond my Earthly time, so I invest in our relationship. An investment in you is guaranteed to yield an unmeasurable return on my investment. Thank you for another opportunity of grace, forgiveness, help, and sanctification. In the name of Jesus, Amen!

"As the heart panteth after the water brooks, So panteth my

soul after thee, O God. My soul thirsteth for God, for the living God: When shall I come and appear before God?"
Psalm 42:1-2 KJV

# DAILY REFLECTIONS

*Today I am grateful for...*

_____
_____
_____

*Today's message reminded that...*

_____
_____
_____

*Today I will strengthen my relationship with God by...*

_____
_____
_____

# DAY 19

Father,
   Learning to depend on you as my source for everything is an ongoing lesson. When I am overwhelmed, I depend on you for calm. When I am hurt, I depend on you for comfort. When I am disappointed and burdened, I depend on you to carry the load and for this, I thank you. You are the source of my strength, my life, and my everything!

What an honor to have you, Lord, as the constant in my life. You are the one who will never fail me. Even when it feels like you let me down, I know that everything will be alright. Everything that happens in me, to me, and for me will work out for my good in the end. Therefore, I rest in the test. Thank you, Lord, for continuously making me a better servant! Regardless of who does or who doesn't, you Lord, are my confidence and I trust in you.

## Meditative Moment

Have you ever been hurt by someone close to you or betrayed by someone who vowed to love you? In an instant, a circumstance or a disagreement quickly changed that promise and you found yourself wounded, betrayed, bewildered and wondering how this happened. Well, we all have been there. Usually, it comes from those who you are closest too! One thing is for certain, two things for sure, Jesus the faithful one will never betray or hurt you. Just run to Him for safety. For He promised us that He will shield us and keep us from hurt and harm.

Today, reflect on how God has brought you through the hurts and disappointments of life. In your journal make note of those times and keep them near to encourage you on the days you feel you can't make it through. Remember, God's word is true, and He is always with us.

## Prayer

Father God, in the name of Jesus, help me today to cast every concern, heartbreak, and dilemma at your feet. Help me to leave them that I may keep pressing forward. It's for my benefit and your glory. Thank you so much for your care. Amen!

> "Cast thy burden upon the LORD, and he shall sustain thee:
> He shall never suffer the righteous to be moved."
> Psalm 55:22 KJV

# DAILY REFLECTIONS

*Today I am grateful for...*

_____
_____
_____

*Today's message reminded that...*

_____
_____
_____

*Today I will strengthen my relationship with God by...*

_____
_____
_____

# DAY 20

Father,
    Today, I am not my best. I love hard and want to do the best by and for people, but it is not always reciprocated. I give and give and pour and pour, and in return it is not always favorable. I lay my heart at your feet, and I ask for you to help me. LORD, please give me peace in my mind and heart. When my heart is overwhelmed, lead me to the rock that is higher than me.

You are the source of my strength and life. Help me to be still and wait on a change—it may not be in the situation but a change in me. Lord, you know I desire to live this life your way. I know that every day won't be easy, so help me to do what I can, when I can, and leave the rest to you. Your best is what I desire and being a reflection of that is what I strive for daily. I need you! Help me, because in my own strength, I cannot do it.

## Meditative Moment

Many of us have gone through where people have mistreated or misused us, and we felt like we were going to go off. I must admit, I have been there, and it truly took the Lord to keep me during those trying times. We must draw close to God in "peace times" so when war times come in our lives, we will be ready and able to hear the Holy Ghost and obey. Whether it's be still and quiet or stand and contend for your faith, you want to hear God clearly.

Today take a moment to look back at times when you didn't listen or couldn't hear because of your anger or disappointment. Take note of ways you could have responded better or postured yourself to hear God's instructions clearly. Learn from those times and prepare for the next, for there surely will be another test.

## Prayer

Help me Jesus! Father God, keep me from falling and present me faultless. If there be any wrong done to me, help me to rise above it all. Lord, may I stay in a humble state for your Divine glory, honor and praise. Thank you for your love and example. In Jesus' name Amen.

> "Hear my cry, O God; Attend unto my prayer. From the end of the earth will I cry unto thee, When my heart is overwhelmed: Lead me to the rock that is higher than I."
> Psalm 61:1-2 KJV

# DAILY REFLECTIONS

*Today I am grateful for...*

_____
_____
_____

*Today's message reminded that...*

_____
_____
_____

*Today I will strengthen my relationship with God by...*

_____
_____
_____

## DAY 21

Father,

The people of God face so much opposition. Many issues of life come to distract and take us off our road to victory. Jesus, I pray for the encouragement of the Saints all around the world. I pray that they will dig deeper and push through like never before to fulfill their purpose in you. Help us to go "All in," and launch out into the deep!

This letter to you is for my sisters and brothers. We need your strength today, Father. Strengthen our hearts and help us to see clearly the matters of our heart. Straighten my life and the life of the one who is reading this. We are learning to lean and depend on you totally, without hesitation or fear.

Walking by faith can sometimes be a scary and uneasy thing, but if we continue to walk, talk, and look to you, we will gain courage. We will be victorious, and we will reach that high prize that we strive for day by day. Help me. No, help us. Lord, you know, and we trust you.

## Meditative Moment

Sometimes we have opposition and struggles that come into our lives that cause us to be fearful and back up. The fear slows us down, and sometimes causes us to miss our "due date" or even worse, miss the opportunity altogether. We must stand knowing that God did not give us a spirit of fear (2 Timothy 1:7). He won't lead us astray or lead us down the wrong path.

Today, reflect on the things in your life that have been causing you to be fearful. Surrender them to God in prayer, and in exchange ask for His peace, joy, and confidence. Remember, God will not abandon you or fail you. Lay your burdens at the feet of the Father, and he will take care of you.

## Prayer

Father God, in the name of Jesus, help us to trust in you! You are our source, and you are for us and not against us. We know that you love us and would not set us up to fail. Help us have the courage to stand for you no matter what it looks like. Strengthen our hand against the opposition and enemy of our life. We know that you have our best interest in mind, and that with you on our side nothing can stand against us. In the name of Jesus Christ, Amen.

"So we say with confidence, The Lord is my helper; I will not be afraid. What can mere mortals do to me?"
Hebrews 13:6, KJV

# DAILY REFLECTIONS

*Today I am grateful for...*

_____
_____
_____

*Today's message reminded that...*

_____
_____
_____

*Today I will strengthen my relationship with God by...*

_____
_____
_____

# DAY 22

Father,
I want to be Right, Real, and Ready. Nothing else matters—NOTHING OR ANYONE. If I am not in right relationship with you, real with how I feel towards you and your people, and ready when you call my name, then my living will be in vain. I cannot afford to worry about the thoughts, feelings, opinions, and even words of others when it comes to being obedient to you. I want to hear you clearly and be clear on your will for me.

My purpose is to praise you, keep your commandments, and obey your every word. Jesus, I can never reach a level of satisfaction here on earth because this earthly vessel is not able to contain the fullness of who you are. So, I keep striving, pushing, praying, and believing. You are the son of God, my savior, my deliverer, my way-maker, my need meeter, my friend, and my source. YOU ARE MY EVERYTHING!

## Meditative Moment

Have you ever felt that you're just not "there yet," or nowhere near where you need to or should be in God? Well, I'm here to tell you that is a great place to be. You never want to get to a place where you feel you're "good" and have reached the pinnacle of your walk with Christ. The place where you can just cruise or ride on off into the sunset of eternity. No, we must keep pushing daily to be Right, Real, and Ready for the return of our Lord and Savior.

Today, take an assessment of your life and relationship with God. Have you become too comfortable? If so, meditate on the ways that you have gotten comfortable and work diligently to get back on track in your pursuit of Right relationship with God. For only what you do for the kingdom of God will last.

## Prayer

Lord, we never want to get to a state of satisfaction with you. We want to keep a longing in our hearts, as the deer pants for the water brook. May our souls long for you all the more. Help us to be the vessel of honor that you desire. In the end, may I stand before you and hear you say, "Well done, thy good and faithful servant," as you welcome me home. In Jesus Christ name we pray, Amen.

> "Let us hear the conclusion of the whole matter: Fear God, and keep his commandments: for this is the whole duty of man."
> Ecclesiastes 12:13 KJV

# DAILY REFLECTIONS

*Today I am grateful for...*

_____
_____
_____

*Today's message reminded that...*

_____
_____
_____

*Today I will strengthen my relationship with God by...*

_____
_____
_____

# DAY 23

Father,
Life can be so different. In my circle of friends, at any given time, we can each be experiencing a different stage of life at the same time. One may be going through promotions and increase, while another sickness and unrest, and yet another the sudden death of a loved one. However, in all of this Lord, you are the constant stabilizer in the middle of it all. I give you praise for being my hiding place, my strength, my covering in good and bad times. You even kept me when I didn't know danger was lurking around the corner.

You are my CONSTANT! Constant friend, constant provider, constant confidant, constant teacher, and I appreciate you for never changing. Things and seasons may change around me; but you, oh Lord, remain the same, and your word never changes. You said what you meant, and it is up to me to follow it. So today, I say yes to the truth. I say yes to the God of all creation!

Please continue to be my fortress and my guide! I put all my trust in you. I am your willing vessel. Please mold and shape me as you see fit. I surrender my heart to love as you say love, to help my neighbor, to treat others with respect, and to be a constant reflection of you. If I want to be like you Jesus, I must put on your characteristics and follow Your example. So, Lord, create in me a Jesus heart! A heart that forgives, loves, and shows mercy.

### Meditative Moment

Think about who Jesus is. Do you know that He has never changed his character? He may have mercy and change his mind because of our prayers, but his character never changes. He never fails, he never lies, and we can be sure that he doesn't want us too either. It is not his will that we perish, because He loves us.

Today, let's be mindful to keep allowing God to be and stay that constant stabilizer in our lives as we continue through this life.

### Prayer

Father God, in the name of Jesus, we come to you with open hands and an open heart. Remove every false thing within us from the root. Lord, help us to grow in your love, grace, fruit, and power that we may be a witness unto others of your constant stability. Lord, may our hearts be fertile ground to your love, will, and direction. Let nothing that is not of you take root in our hearts. We trust your will and your plan for our lives, and we say Yes to you today. In the mighty name of Jesus, Amen.

"Search me, O God, and know my heart: Try me, and know my thoughts: And see if there be any wicked way in me, And lead me in the way everlasting."
Psalm 139:23-24 KJV

# DAILY REFLECTIONS

*Today I am grateful for...*

_____
_____
_____

*Today's message reminded that...*

_____
_____
_____

*Today I will strengthen my relationship with God by...*

_____
_____
_____

# DAY 24

Father,
Sometimes I wonder why you want to spend time with me, especially when you're always with me. You know me better than I know myself, yet you want me to set aside time to come and communicate with you daily. Lord, pull me into you, into your loving arms and your wonderful grace so that I can be satisfied in my soul. I totally depend on you all day, every day, and want to dwell in your presence. You bring me life.

Let me continue to share in your joy as you sanctify me for your glory through and through. Let my life reflect my time with you. Let Your love overflow from my countenance and may it abide always in my heart, even when others seem hard to love. May the love of Jesus Christ bubble over continuously in my life.

### Meditative Moment

Have you ever said that you wanted to be like Jesus? Have you considered what that truly means? Jesus displayed love, wisdom, and faithfulness even when others despised and begrudged him. To be like Jesus means to spend time in the Father's presence communing with him, following his instructions, and loving your brothers and sisters unconditionally.

Today let's pray for God's grace and mercy, and that he will help us to love like Jesus. Then, let's practice demonstrating the love of Jesus toward those we encounter today.

### Prayer

Father God, in the name of Jesus, thank you for the opportunity to be in a closer relationship with you. Starting today, I will intentionally make time to spend in your presence walking and talking with you throughout my day. I will not look at this time as an obligation, chore, or duty, but as a joy and privilege. Freely I come and spend time in your presence. May I never know what it is to be lost without you. In the name of Jesus, Amen.

> "O love the LORD, all ye his saints: For the LORD preserveth the faithful, and plentifully rewardeth the proud doer. Be of good courage, and he shall strengthen your heart,
> All ye that hope in the LORD."
> Psalm 31:23-24 KJV

# DAILY REFLECTIONS

*Today I am grateful for...*

_____
_____
_____

*Today's message reminded that...*

_____
_____
_____

*Today I will strengthen my relationship with God by...*

_____
_____
_____

# DAY 25

Father,
    Thank you for the gift of salvation and grace. Freely you give unto me, even when I am unworthy! You bless me and have fellowship and sweet communication with me. I accept your continuous invitation to be in your presence and be one with you. You listen to me and allow me to share my heart in every situation and circumstance. You have given a gift to me that I did not earn nor can ever repay to you.

Your love, your grace, and your mercy are truly greater than life itself. Help me Jesus get this love thing right, so I too can not only receive grace, but give grace to my sisters and brothers without looking for anything in return. I don't deserve it and maybe they don't either, but I will make it my mission to show God's love, grace, and mercy to others, just as it has been shown to me. Lord, I want to know you in an intimate way where your love flows through me to someone who needs you. Your grace is absolutely wonderful and appreciated. Thank you!

### Meditative Moment

Can you think of a time in your life when you deserved punishment, but instead you were forgiven? Maybe you were a child and your actions deserved far greater than the stern talking too that you received. That was a form of grace, or better yet, mercy. God often gives us more than once to correct our behavior and disobedience when he could very well punish us the first time. Through grace, he continues to bless and provide for us. In his mercy, he spares us of the harsh punishment we deserved.

Today, be a reflection of God and be sure to extend grace and mercy to those that have hurt or caused you offense. Also, don't forget to take time to thank God for this experience in life. We often deserve death, but God's grace and mercy keeps us.

### Prayer

Father, in the name of Jesus, thank you! Thank you! Thank you! These are the only words that come to mind when we think of your goodness. No other words can truly express our gratitude for the renewed grace and mercy we receive daily. We give our lives completely over to you. Touch our hearts that we not only receive grace, but also give grace. Thank you for your love, grace, and mercy. In the name of Jesus, Amen.

"For by grace are ye saved through faith; and that not of yourselves: it is the gift of God:"
Ephesians 2:8 KJV

# DAILY REFLECTIONS

*Today I am grateful for...*

_____
_____
_____

*Today's message reminded that...*

_____
_____
_____

*Today I will strengthen my relationship with God by...*

_____
_____
_____

## DAY 26

Father,

When I think of your goodness and greatness, and the many times you have brought me through life's situations and circumstances, I owe you my life. I know that we are not saved by the works that we do, but I just want to show my appreciation for your love. When I was a child, I wanted my Daddy to be proud of me. So, I did my best and made decisions I knew would make Him smile and proud to call me his daughter. Father, for you I want to do that and more. I want to make you smile and be proud of my service unto you.

What an absolute honor to be able to please the King of kings—the one who spoke, and everything came into existence. Lord, you are awesome! Draw my heart to yours. Let my life be an example of your goodness. I yearn to be better and pleasing in your sight. No one else matters. No one can keep me, heal me, or touch me at my core, satisfying my soul.

You were the missing piece. When I was lost, you were "that thing" I was searching for. Then, you called me. It was a loving and holy call, one that I am so glad I chose to answer. You have charted my life ever since. Lord, you are so good!

## Meditative Moment

If you were privileged to grow up with a parent, or both parents, did you want to make them happy? I know I did. I was not always an obedient child, but I wanted to make my parents smile. In this life we will have trouble, but our Father has already overcome this world through his son Jesus Christ. If we lean into God and his plan for our lives, how pleased do you think he would be with us and our lives?

Today, let's look to our Heavenly Father and ask Him what is it he would have us to do at this place in our lives? What better way to bring a smile to his face, then seeking out his will for our lives. When we are obedient to God's plan, the reward is far greater than we can imagine. So, meditate on His word and spend time listening for his voice so that you may know what he wants you to do.

## Prayer

Lord, we long to be what you want us to be. We want you to be pleased with our lives. Clean us up from the inside out! Rest in us and on us! We give you permission to saturate our hearts with your love and help us to reflect your love. You are God and no one else is higher than you.

We place you on the throne of our hearts, and we lift you

up within our lives. Thank you for the opportunity to bless you and make you smile. We want to be obedient children, ready to be used by you, mighty God. We want to make you proud. Help us day by day, minute by minute, moment by moment. In the name of Jesus, Amen.

> "Whosoever shall seek to save his life shall lose it; and whosoever shall lose his life shall preserve it."
> Luke 17:33 KJV

# DAILY REFLECTIONS

*Today I am grateful for...*

_____
_____
_____

*Today's message reminded that...*

_____
_____
_____

*Today I will strengthen my relationship with God by...*

_____
_____
_____

# DAY 27

Father,
    Thank you Jesus, for Peace! The peace that you left for your children. All we have to do is rest in your peace. Today, regardless of what's going on, I choose peace. I choose a righteous mind. I choose unshakeable faith! May the peace in my heart continuously flow from my lips.

Lord, help me stay the course and do what's right in your eyes, rather than focusing on "being the right one." Families and friends have broken up because someone wouldn't humble themselves. Countries have been divided, and people lost their lives due to pride. I want you, Father, to be happy and pleased with me and my life. Therefore, I am choosing to not focus on being the one that's right, but rather the one that's doing right according to you. Peace, I call you to rule in my heart because it is what is in my heart that matters.

### Meditative Moment

Peace, so many people have forfeited their peace and the peace of others, just to be right. Let's keep in mind that everything we do and say is being recorded by our Heavenly Father. Our goal and objective should be to please Him, the one that can destroy and save our souls. Let us reverently fear our maker and choose peace over conflict.

Today, think about a recent situation where you allowed your pride to cause a divide. Ask God how you can restore the relationship and his peace. Then ask for the courage to follow through.

### Prayer

Lord Jesus, when things get heated and out of order, please help us to choose peace above being right or heard. If our hearts are saturated with your peace and your word, our tongues can be tamed and not rule over us. For the tongue speaks what is in our hearts. So Lord, cultivate our hearts with forgiveness and sweet peace that we may be an example to this dying world. Thank you for your peace, in the name of Jesus Christ, Amen.

> "And let the peace of God rule in your hearts, to the which also ye are called in one body; and be ye thankful."
> Colossians 3:15 KJV

# DAILY REFLECTIONS

*Today I am grateful for...*

_____
_____
_____

*Today's message reminded that...*

_____
_____
_____

*Today I will strengthen my relationship with God by...*

_____
_____
_____

# DAY 28

Father,
 Awesome ruler, mighty counselor, my peace, my strength, my constant, my way-maker, my hope, my guide, my sustainer, my safety, and my everything! I am so grateful to have said Yes to you! I am grateful to have been called and loved by you! I want to take advantage of this time, this grace, this opportunity to give you Glory and honor, and to put you first in my life once again! I surrender my heart to you, once again, and completely lay my life down for you. Use me!

Holy Ghost, take over in my heart and mind. In my relationship with you, help me to never give into complacency or allow self- righteousness to rise up in my heart. I pray that haughtiness, pride, and sin stay far away from me. I pray that your manifested presence, anointing, grace, and love are always with me. You said that those who are not yours on that day, you will say, "I never knew you!" I want you to know me and my name. I pray that I live a life pleasing to you and that my name is written in the lamb's book of life! Nothing else matters. NOTHING!!!!

## Meditative Moment

How bad do you want to make it? Not here on this earth, but in that number that John saw, which was so great he could not even count. Why don't we commit today to not do anything, willingly or intentionally, that would cause God to say he never knew us. The Fruit of the Spirit must be evident and working in our lives daily.

Today, let's eat the fruit of love, joy, peace, longsuffering, gentleness, goodness, faith, meekness, and temperance. When we eat of this fruit, we will have no law against us.

## Prayer

Father God, in the name of Jesus, we surrender all to you! Our entire life is in your hand. Lord, keep us in the center of your will, not looking for an excuse to sin or trying to find a loophole to do what we want to do. Help us to follow your word and defend against evil. May we be presented as holy vessels unto you. Tear down and cleanse us of any self-righteousness and grant us a humble heart and contrite spirit. We want to dwell with you when we leave this life, so please help us. In the name of Jesus, Amen.

"Be not thou therefore ashamed of the testimony of our Lord, nor of me his prisoner: but be thou partaker of the afflictions of the gospel according to the power of God; who

hath saved us, and called us with an holy calling, not according to our works, but according to his own purpose and grace, which was given us in Christ Jesus before the world began,"
2 Timothy 1:8-9 KJV

# DAILY REFLECTIONS

*Today I am grateful for...*

_____
_____
_____

*Today's message reminded that...*

_____
_____
_____

*Today I will strengthen my relationship with God by...*

_____
_____
_____

# DAY 29

*F*ather,
When I look back over my life, I can see how your hand of protection has guided me. If I had gone left, it would possibly have been the end for me. Had I not said yes to you, it would not have been the same outcome. My end would have come. Father God, I THANK YOU for ordering my steps! I'm glad I was obedient to your call and did it your way!

As I continue forward, help me to stay on the straight and narrow path of righteousness. Help me to fix and focus my eyes on you alone. Not looking to the left, right, or behind me, but looking up to you and moving forward on this pilgrimage—being obedient to your every word and command. You have my best interest in mind. Bid me to come closer, and I will come.

I want to learn at your feet and reflect your light. Who am I to say who does or does not deserve grace? The same grace you extend to me, I shall extend to others as you so direct. For without your grace, I would be sentenced to a burning hell right now. I bless and thank you for an obedient heart, and I pray that I continue to have a heart of forgiveness, obedience, and love. Life with You is my goal. May you never leave my view. I need you, Jesus!

### Meditative Moment

What is important to you? When you're alone in a situation with no one else to help you, where do you turn? On the other side of this life that we currently know, no one but God can go with you. He is with us from the beginning and on to our end spiritually. So, why not seek to please Him? Let us purpose in our hearts and minds to bless and please our wonderful Father with our lives. Let us strive for a closer walk daily with him as we study and meditate on His word.

Today, think of ways to spend time with God throughout the day. Maybe join a daily prayer group to stay connected to the source of your strength. He desires more of you, so why not give yourself completely to him?

### Prayer

Father, in the name of Jesus, give us a hunger and thirst for you like never before. Give us a burning desire to be more like you, and help us to stray away from evil thoughts, deeds, and an evil heart. We want to be simple, pure, sincere and real with you. We want to align with your will for our lives. Your way is the best way. We don't want to deviate from your plan, so we say yes, yes, yes! We need more of you. We freely surrender to you and worship giving you total praise because YOU ARE GOD! Thank you, thank you, thank you! In the name of Jesus, Amen.

"Wherefore take unto you the whole armour of God, that ye may be able to withstand in the evil day, and having done all, to stand."
Ephesians 6:13 KJV

# DAILY REFLECTIONS

*Today I am grateful for...*

_____
_____
_____

*Today's message reminded that...*

_____
_____
_____

*Today I will strengthen my relationship with God by...*

_____
_____
_____

# DAY 30

Father,
I want to always have an attitude of gratitude! Never complaining or not being content with what you have provided for me. I want my heart to be in a place where thanksgiving always flows. My heart says, "Thank you Lord!" Jesus, without you, I would be nothing! I would be lost with no hope. I am thankful for another opportunity to come to you and ask for forgiveness. I give you all the praise and glory!

My relationship with you is so important to me, and I want you to know my name. Lord your will is not bondage, it's freedom! Freedom to know that I have hope and safety in you. I am grateful that I even have a mind to press into your presence through praise and prayer.

Now, help me say yes tomorrow, and the next day, and the day after that, and so on until you call me home. Nothing else matters, and nothing is as important as you and I building and growing together! What an awesome God you are. You give me opportunities again and again to come to you, boldly without reservation, and get it right. It's a privilege to come before you, the God of all creation, the God of time, and the God of my salvation.

Make me better! Shape and mold me. May my love and longing for you grow daily. Only you can help me. I love you Lord! I need you Lord, and I want to grow in you. This is why I wrote to you these love letters, that you may see how much I love and desire to be the best version me for the glory of Your Kingdom.

### Meditative Moment

Isn't our God good? When you reflect on your life, do you remember the times you veered off path and God reeled you back into His safety? God doesn't want us to fail. He has already designed it for us to win, but we must be willing to be open and honest with Him. After all, he already knows our thoughts before we think them.

Today, let's make a commitment to be diligent and press into the will and presence of God seeking His face. We must become who He has purposed and created us to be. Give God permission to make you, shape you, revive you, and renew you. Say YES to him, yielding and surrendering every day!

### Prayer

Father, in the name of Jesus. There is nothing more important than the salvation of our souls and serving out our God given purposes. We want you to have the right of way in our hearts and minds. We give you a yes today, tomorrow, and every day to come, that we may be pleasing in your sight. Heaven is our goal, a reflection of Jesus is our aim, and the Victory is ours if we continue to abide in you. We love you and appreciate your guidance throughout our lifetime. The straight and narrow way is the path we will take because that is where you have called us to. We say Yes to your will, and Yes to your way! We thank you and appreciate you. In the name of Jesus, Amen.

"I press toward the mark for the prize of the high calling of God in Christ Jesus."
Philippians 3:14 KJV

# DAILY REFLECTIONS

*Today I am grateful for...*

_____
_____
_____

*Today's message reminded that...*

_____
_____
_____

*Today I will strengthen my relationship with God by...*

_____
_____
_____

# THE GIFT OF SALVATION

Salvation is a free gift from God, and all we have to do to receive it is trust and believe that Jesus is who he said he is. Romans 10:9-15 reminds us that if we confess with our mouths and believe in our hearts that God raised Jesus from the dead, we shall be saved. It's that simple.

The Anti-Christ movement is upon us. In these times, we must stick to the blueprint established by God the Father and actively pursue God through prayer and relationship like never before so we may be ready for the Messiah's return. Let us put away division, strife, jealousy, and any other feeling within our hearts that is not of God, and let us be about our Father's business witnessing to those around us. Each one, reach one, then teach one as we live a life that is a great example of a follower of Christ.

Write your love letters to God and seek His face daily. If you haven't asked him into your heart, pour out your heart before Him and give Him a try. We can make it together, taking it one day and one soul at a time. We may not be able to save THE world, but we can help save someone in OUR world, those we encounter. Let Jesus be your guide, and let's live this life righteously, wholeheartedly, and Holy. Until we meet again here on Earth or the other side of Glory, stay laser focused on Jesus, and let's win souls for the Kingdom of God.

# ABOUT THE AUTHOR

Alaina Hunt grew up in the small town of Goose Creek, South Carolina. There, she was taught the life lessons of hard work and staying humble.

In 1996, she joined the United States Army to explore the world and broaden her knowledge of people. In 2001, she moved to Maryland, by way of the military, and found love. There, she began to build her life with her husband and church family. From her union with her husband, Maurice,

God blessed them with 4 loving children, Simone, Stephen, Shane, and Salena, whom she is so proud of.

Alaina is now a disabled veteran working for the Lord. She strives to be the best daughter and servant unto God, the best wife to her husband, and the best mother to her children, understanding that they are all watching her walk. She is a licensed Evangelist, and her pursuit and relationship with God is first and foremost. She hopes that her body of work will help others find a place of safety and peace in God.

**THANK YOU!**

www.ingramcontent.com/pod-product-compliance
Lightning Source LLC
Chambersburg PA
CBHW071249070526
44583CB00017B/2395